The Poetic Rhythms of Life

Quincey Bennett

AuthorHouse™
1663 Liberty Drive
Bloomington, IN 47403
www.authorhouse.com
Phone: 1-800-839-8640

Published by AuthorHouse 01/08/2015

ISBN: 978-1-4969-4243-2 (sc)
ISBN: 978-1-4969-4242-5 (e)

Library of Congress Control Number: 2014919681

The Poetic Rhythms of Life

Quincey Bennett

A Child's Wonder

How can the stars shine so bright
In the darkest country night?
Where does the sun get its light
To shine the brightest bright?
Who commands the stars and moon to run and hide
When the sunlight rises to kiss the sky?
A child's wonder.
How can the world be made round
When we're safely planted on the ground?
Who spins it on its axis rotating round and round?
Who knows where the end of the world may be found?
A child's wonder.
Who painted the clouds the whitest whites?
Where does the lightning bug get its light?
And who painted the butterfly's wings?
And what makes the red bird sing?
Just how wide are the eagle's wings?
A child's wonder.
What makes the bumblebee sting?
And who crowned the lion king?
God is the answer to all these things.

A Dear Friend Is Gone but Not Forgotten

A dear friend is gone.

When will I stop crying?

I'm wondering why time took you away.

Who will fill this void of empty space?

It seems my smile's been taken from my face.

Where's the joy and the laughter?

Life sometimes brings such disaster.

I cannot conceive or my heart believe that my dear friend's not here.

You were my love, my dear dear friend,

A friend that God has sent.

And so I call to Him,

Attend to me, oh Lord, my heart's been broken.

It seems my friend's been stolen.

Mend my heart of this hurting.

How can I go on, oh Lord?

How can I be strong

When it feels all hope is gone?

How can I sing that brand-new song?

I can't heal on my own.

So heal me with your healing balm.

I cry to you,

For all life's remedies lie in you.

A Shifting in the Spirit

There's a shifting in the spirit,
A subtle change in the atmosphere.
Favor and blessings are what I hear,
A blessing of health and tremendous wealth
Is headed in my direction.
The word of
God declares that it shall be.
Yes, my blessings are coming to me.
All my bills are paid,
My children are saved,
The shift has caused my enemies to be at peace with me,
A footstool to rest my feet.
In my life, there's no defeat, no lack, no need.
I have all that I need;
At the sound of God's word, I am complete.

A Son Is Gone

My heart aches for the mother and father that lost their son;
A terrible injustice has been done.
Shot in the heart, his life is taken.
I know his mother's heart is breaking.
I pray for her, her eyes flooding with tears;
Her child's been taken in such short years.
Another life is gone
With just one bullet from a gun.
A loving mother and father lost their son.
He's just one too many gone so soon.
I cry and weep with tears.
I feel the pain of their suffering and loss;
To lose a child, what a priceless cost.
Another soul is gone,
Never again to return home.
His laugh and cry never to be heard again;
A life has come to a needless end.
How will the parents ever heal?
God and time will reveal.
Yes, they too in time will heal,
Because there's no sorrow heaven can't heal.

A Treasured Friendship

I found a treasure in you;
It doesn't matter what others may say.
Real friendships sparkle behind cloudy skies,
Put joy and gladness in my eyes.
You're a true and loving friend.
Time with you is well spent,
Like fond memories from a distant past.
A friendship in you shall long outlast
Acquaintances that come and go.
Lord, you're a friend indeed.
You surpass boundaries and limits.
You stick closer than the dearest brothers;
You far surpass any others.
You're faithful as well as true;
Life's assurance rests in you.
You'll take me where I need to go,
Teach me all I need to know.
Without you, oh Lord,
Where shall I go?
You're the only help I know.
You'll long outlast present, past, and future.
You're an eternal friend.
You understand my weakness.
You understand my strengths.
Lord, you foreknew me.
You're that treasured friend.

A Virtuous Mother

A mother's heart is so endearing

When her heart is God-fearing.

She's a treasure to her children.

It's mama's praying hands that help shape the world.

She's a vessel of wisdom to every boy and girl.

God entrusted a mother to be a bearer of good things;

There's life, love, and virtue in all she brings.

She's a gift from God up above;

A mother's filled with warmth and forgiveness.

God has created her so unique;

She's wisdom in all she speaks.

She's serves her children in humility;

Patience, she's been given plenty.

She wears a fragrance called tranquility.

She's a supplier of her children's needs.

Her hands are gifted with healing.

Her mouth an instrument of praise.

She shall be blessed in all her days.

She rebukes but rebuilds.

She speaks with wisdom and clarity.

She shares the greatest gift of charity.

Acknowledge the Lord

In all my days, I will acknowledge you
For all the wonders that you do.
I will acknowledge you with praise upon my lips;
It's you, oh God, I will uplift.
I live and breathe because of you.
My life, my strength, they lie in you.
I am aware of your loving grace,
Each morning I rise to wash my face.
You permissioned me a brand-new day;
I thank you with breath-given praise.
It was you that caused the sun to shine;
You had me on your mind.
I acknowledge you for the bounty of love you show to all each day,
For the many blessings you send our way.
I will forever give thanks to you
For the clothes you provide upon my back,
For each piece hung upon my closet's rack.
I acknowledge you that I am not naked and bare;
Thank you, Lord, for always being there.
Thank you for the shoes upon my feet,
Protection from rocks and gravel underneath.
Thank you for my sweater and hat—
Yes, oh Lord, you did all that.
I acknowledge you
For all the awesomeness you do.

Believe in Yourself

I keep telling you that you're great;

When will you arise and walk with faith?

I keep telling you that I believe in you;

When will you arise and believe in yourself?

I keep telling you that you can accomplish your dreams;

Is this an empty song that I sing?

I keep telling you that you're amazing;

It's your true character that I'm praising.

I keep telling you that you can fly;

Spread your wings of faith and try.

Stop doubting yourself, believe and fly.

I keep telling you, my son,

Against all odds with God's help you've already won.

Blank Canvas

The artist gathered His canvas,
Its surface dark and bare, not an element of life found anywhere.
There was no light, only the blackness of the void,
But in an instance, void was destroyed.
He created the essence of light,
The Earth was filled, light revealed;
The stars, sun, and the moon flooded their light.
The word was spoke, void was broke, and darkness disbanded.
The earth was created, the water abated, all was new and updated.
The world began, creation invaded.
The waters gathered, creating oceans, lakes and streams.
All was good to the artist, it seemed.
In His heart and soul, the artist was pleased.
Oh, what a tempest song the waters sing.
The sun and moon he hung high.
Its violet rays bursting forth from the sky.
What a beautiful world came to be;
God the creator created thee.
From the words of His mouth, creation was born.
Creation's beauty was adorned.

Comfortable in My Own Skin

Comfortable in the skin I'm in.
I must never be ashamed
Of my origin from where I came.
I'm proud of my Negro-African name;
I wear a broad and beautiful frame;
I'm proud of my large almond eyes,
The clash of thunder in my thighs,
The smoothness in my stride;
I'm proud of the wideness of my heart-shaped hips,
The fullness of my lips.
I'm wonderfully and uniquely made.
I'm the only me there is,
The only me I can give,
The me in which I live.
I'm comfortable in my own skin black and silky,
Proud of my curly-kinky hair.
Wow! I have such a flair.
Love me if you dare.
Embrace my complexion, dark and fair.
When you see me walking, chin lifted high,
My body position towering to the sky.
I'm proud of the skin I'm in.
I am genuine no need for disguise.
I'm a black, full-figured girl.
I'm an asset to this world.
I am black and I am strong.
I am the music to my song.
I'm comfortable in the skin I'm in.

Complainers

Complainers complain about everything,

The same sad song they always sing.

That have a spirit that will sift you dry,

Put boohoo tears in your eyes.

So direct the complainer to a life of prayer

When life doesn't seem to be going well.

Complainers will always stay the same,

For all they do is complain.

If all you do is complain,

Nothing in your life will ever change.

Dare to Stand

Dare to stand when you seem to stand alone;

Dare to stand when all your hope seems to be gone.

Dare to stand with a true friend;

Dare to stand when true friendships come to an end.

Dare to stand when life and you are at your best;

Dare to stand when facing life's greatest test.

Dare to stand when life's rains are pouring;

Dare to stand when life's seas are roaring.

Dare to stand when faced with enemies;

Dare to stand when faced with intellectual indignities.

Dare to stand in opposition;

Dare to stand in life's blurred visions.

Dare to stand—stay on the mission;

Dare to stand when in transition.

Dare to stand when the odds are against you.

Dare to stand knowing this one thing:

That God is for you.

Destiny Awaits You

How hard you try
Determines how high you fly.
Stay true to yourself.
Your own efforts propel and excel;
You are your own fuel.
You have all you need to succeed.
Push and encourage yourself,
Not relying on anyone else.
As you chase you purposed destiny,
Avoid the temptation of hate and greed.
Stay true.
Stay honest.
You will succeed.
Stay true to your soul.
Stick to your goal.
Stay true to the instinct of your soul.
Don't be defeated when the road you're traveling seems all uphill—
Your destiny awaits you still.
When obstacles obstruct your way,
You set the pace.
Take that leap of faith.
You will clear every obstacle in your way.
You're moving closer to your goal;
You can feel it in your soul.
Don't be defeated by "friends" or foes;
There are higher heights that you must go.
Spread your wings and soar,
Soar beyond the sky.
Stay focused in your mind,
For it's by your own thoughts that you are defined.

Do the Opposite

Do the opposite of what some may expect.

When expected to hate, confuse the enemy by showing love.

When expected to back down,

Be courageous and stand your ground.

When expected to doubt, have faith to believe.

When expected to give up, press on to achieve.

When expected to retaliate, strive to keep the bond of peace.

When expected to cry, let out a loud, hearty laugh.

When things go wrong, just keep pressing on.

When expected to fail, believe and prevail.

When thrown in life's fires,

Sing a song to inspire.

When placed in life's prison,

Maintain your vision.

When placed in your lion's den,

Wait for divine intervention.

When the odds are against you,

Know that I, God, am for you.

I'm Driven by You

It's your love, dear Lord, that inspires me;
You're that internal flame that drives me.
It's your power that gives me strength.
It's to you, oh Lord, that I pray and vent.
It's through your grace that I am able to stand.
I'm held strong by your mighty hand.
In my enemies' plot, you had a plan.
You allow me to defeat my enemies.
It's your love that entreats me.
You hold me up; you delivered me.
In all my days, I'll be led and driven by you.

Earth's Fatherless Child

Where is your father?
Where did he go?
What does he look like?
Do you even know?
I know I'm His child,
His very own.
I'm flesh of His flesh;
I'm bone of His bone.
Why didn't he reach out to me?
It seemed he never tried.
He made it seem just like my earth father had died.
It was never a maybe;
I am His baby.
So why would he leave
His blood, body, and soul?
It's certainly sad;
Sometimes I'm really still mad.
He took away my rights to having a dad.
He missed all my birthdays, every holiday,
And at my wedding, he didn't give me away.

"So, mama, what did I do to make my daddy leave you?
Was I a bad kid?
Was it something I did?
Oh, mama, please tell me;
I want to make it right.
I just want my dad to be a part of my life."
"Earth's fatherless child, you are never alone.
I am your heavenly father, and you are my own.
Earth's fatherless child, why don't you dry up those tears?
Give me all of your fears.
I am your heavenly father,
And you are my own."

Extreme Testing

In the case of extreme testing,
Our faith is put on trial.
The duration of the test we cannot tell,
Though sometimes the testing seems like hell.
Extreme testing measures our strengths,
Perfects our weaknesses.
In many cases, the testing completes.
It's a test of endurance, of our blessed assurance.
In this testing we will find, is victory truly mine?
While going through it, it seems we're walking alone;
Rest assured—Jesus is still on the throne.
We began to wonder, "Where are my friends and family?"
I'm not offended; I know in my soul the test is for me.
I think, "Will I pass, or will I fail?"
Knowing deep in my soul I will prevail.
Knowing in my test God is simply investing a new anointing.
He's appointing authority and standard.
And so I must put forth my best; through God's power I will pass the test.
God will manifest blessed assurance.

Faith's Current

Faith, like the currents, is strong and unending;

Faith on limited sight is never depending.

Its currents flow far beyond what the naked eye can see.

Faith strengthens by purpose and divine destiny.

Faith: the substance of things hoped for, evidence not seen;

Never performs on sight's abilities.

New boundaries and territories faith does explore.

There's no limitation to those that believe and work hard to achieve.

Faith's currents flow strong in the man that possesses it.

Through faith we can do all things, to all that possess it.

Forgiveness

In the act of forgiving, I am forgiven.
I am made free of bitterness and my own hate.
In forgiving, vengeance is not my destined fate;
In the hurts of others, I can relate.
In forgiving, I am made strong;
I'm given words to life's greatest song... freedom.
In all life's pain, I've overcome.
In true forgiveness, I'm made truly free,
Not hindered by hate's disabilities.
In forgiving, nothing negative can hold me fast,
Not today, and not my past.
In true forgiveness, hate cannot take a holding grip,
For the song of freedom rests upon my lips.

Free Your Soul

We waste too much time when we fight to be right to usurp control.

Neglecting to show love,

To forgive and console.

Avoiding the underlying issues,

We should seek for answers and try to fix them.

We allow unforgiveness and hate to rot the soul,

Causing our lives to spiral out of control.

Some are damaged in early childhood

By the very ones we love so dear.

And so we experience unforgiveness.

This venom sends our lives in a downward spiral.

Too much pride, it kills one inside.

Robs us of our joy, making life seem void,

Yet we go on existing, not really living.

Unforgiveness turns into hate;

To love and kindness, it becomes hard to relate.

Building up walls, we falter and fall.

Making the same mistakes,

Causing our loved ones' hearts to ache.

To true love and contentment, we become blind;

We should demonstrate love and compassion,

And not to assassin.

Forgive your enemies of all their debts.

By this, you free your soul.

Your enemies have no more control.

Friends Forever

Many years have come and gone;
Our friendship remains true and strong.
We've been through so much together;
Our bond of friendship will last forever.
I'm grateful to God
For sending me a friend like you.
Through years, your love has never changed;
I'm so thankful you remained the same.
You're a friend of true character and soul;
These are important as we grow old.
Friends like you are hard to find;
I'm so thankful that you are mine.
I have so many fond memories of times spent together;
These beautiful memories will last forever.
They're engraved in my heart and soul;
We will still be friends in eternity,
For surely God gave you to me.

Glory to the King

Glory to the king,

Holy and righteous is His name.

Heaven and Earth they all proclaim,

Glory to the living king.

Let us bless His holiness by the shedding of blood he's redeemed us.

Rejoice with me, all ye angels,

Heavenly bearers of light.

Darkness gave way and took its flight.

Glory to God, the master and king, ruler and maker of everything.

Sing with me in worship and praise,

For His great mercy and unmerited grace.

He has risen in my soul;

His joyous salvation has been told.

God Was Always Here

I was before the worlds began.

I am God; I created man.

From the dust of the earth,

Long before a natural birth,

I was before a planet Earth.

I was before time began,

Before lightning, thunder, rain, or sand,

I created the conjunction "and."

And let there be light, and there was light

And darkest nights.

The greater light to rule the day,

The lesser light to rule the night,

Not by power, not by might,

But by my spirit, sayeth the Lord,

For my words are a mighty sword.

I was before any ocean, any sea,

Before Hitchcock wrote a mystery.

I was before any being,

Believing is not always seeing.

I was before the clouds of white,

Even before the bright sunlight.

I was here before forecast lows and highs.

I placed the planets in the sky

Way before planes could fly.

I created life's primary colors,

Indigo, reds, violet, blues,

Before Michelangelo had a clue.

The world itself my work of art,

Before Leonardo Da Vinci got his start.

I Am God; I created art,

The most complicated organ, the heart,

The first computer, the brain,

Every major organ,

Every muscle, nerve, and vein.

Look at yourself and clearly see

Man, my greatest masterpiece.

I created the hemisphere and stratosphere;

I created the atlas and atmosphere.

I was before the dinosaur,

Before the birds that soar.

I was before the lion's roar,

Before any creature crept,

Before the leaping leapt.

I am the Christ, the creator of all.

Where did I come from?

I Am God.

I was always here.

God Will Never Leave You

Like the stars that never leave the sky,
Like the darkness that never leaves the night,
Like the sun sustains its light,
I'll never leave you.
Like the waves that never leave the sea,
Like the wind that never loses its breeze,
Like the snow that never leaves its freeze,
Like the leaves on the evergreens,
I'll never leave you.
Like a baby that never leaves its cry,
Like true love that never dies,
Like the color in your eyes,
Like the motion in the ocean,
I'll never leave you.

God Will Take Care of You

God takes care of His own, so take no thought for tomorrow
Rejoice with gladness, don't live in sorrow
God will take care of you as He takes care of the smallest of birds
He is a keeper of His word
He'll supply your every need
Although the ravens and sparrows never planted a seed
Yet food and water they do reap
Surely God will supply our every need
He feeds the birds a bounty of food
Earthworms, grubs, and all sorts of seeds
A natural buffet with plenty to eat every day of the week
And so as the birds rise early in the morning
Let us arise with great expectation
Looking to receive a harvest from the Lord
Leave all your worries behind
God will supply, just keep in mind
Those that seek will truly find
To all that knock, the door will be opened
Faith's the key; keep on hoping
Remember, take no thought of the food you will eat
Or the clothes you will wear
God has the way already prepared
As God so graciously takes care of the sparrows
How much more will He take care of you
As the birds give praise unto God
Let us rise each day praising Him too
God will take care of you

God's Word

God's word has meaning;
Man's word can't hurt me.
No man can curse me,
So I keep on dreaming.
God's word esteems me,
Builds and protects me,
Defends and heals me,
Makes and molds me,
Breaks and consoles me,
Strengthens in weakness,
Conquers defeat,
Makes demons retreat.
The revealer of mysteries,
Proven through history.
Its soundness unbreakable,
Triumphant and able,
Can accomplish any task,
Cannot be masked, duplicated, or imitated.
It is the unadulterated truth,
Life's most powerful weapon and tool.
Understood by fools,
God's word is forever,
Life's greatest truth.

He Died for All

A man of sorrow, acquainted with grief,
Hung beside a common thief.
Guiltless of doing any wrong,
God the savior went along.
He hung there on that rugged cross,
That a world of sinners would not be lost.
He paid that day a priceless cost.
As a sheep to the slaughter,
He never said a mumbling word,
For the voice of His Father he clearly heard.
He knew the will of His father must be done,
And so on the cross, for three days he hung.
He was the Father's only begotten son.
Begotten out of God,
Given a body in the likeness of men,
Sent to the world to save men from sin.
He was whipped, bruised, and crucified,
Yet with a heart of love for all he died.
He gave up the ghost, accompanied by a heavenly host,
Angels all around commanded not to interfere.
God was about His Father's will.

He Knows It All

To God, I am an open book,
Every cranny, every nook.
My heart is never overlooked.
If I never tell, he knows me well
In this earthly house in which I dwell.
He knows me better than I know myself.
If I should never speak a word,
In all my silence, I'm loudly heard.
He knows the thoughts and hearts of men,
Even those with hidden sins.
Deep secrets of hearts never told,
His awesome power still unfolds.
He knows the mind, body, and spirit of every soul.

He's a Confidential Friend

Although right now your heart is hurting,
God is still yet working ... He's working on your behalf.
He'll see you safely through
All that life has handed you.
God is with you in the storm;
There's safety in His arms.
He's yet a faithful friend.
Confidential and yet true,
He's not forgotten you.
His love's undying and unique.
With no faltering, His love's complete.
He has open arms of wisdom.
He'll complete you with His joy.
For He's a God of mercy,
Has an eternity of grace;
He'll renew the smile upon your face.
So keep your head held high.
Keep walking in the faith.
Take one day at a time,
With your heavenly father, the Great Divine.
He is a confidential friend.

His Masterpiece

His masterpiece is seen in all the earth,
In every life giving birth,
In all the world and all its girth,
In the hidden treasures in the mines,
In all of histories ancient times,
In every rock, mountain,
And water fountain.
It's seen in the lowest of valleys,
In the greenery of trees,
In the countries' beautiful scenes.
In the beauty of the sea,
In every beast and human being.
His masterpiece is seen on the desert's floor,
On every beach and sandy shore
And all that science has explored.
God's the greatest architect;
Designed the world without a sketch.
Upon all the beauty of the world,
God's signature has been etched.

Hush, Little Baby

Hush, little babe, he never cried,
Never opened or blinked your eyes.
So silent and still, you arrived to earth,
The day so silent at your birth.
The pain and agony your mother did feel,
This pain a billion times more real.
"Oh, my baby's been born asleep;
I never dreamed that in this way we would meet."
Oh, what sadness filled the air,
A pain so great, who could bear?
Sometimes life just isn't fair.
Your mother's been left in a world of sadness,
But God will sustain her
Through loss and madness.
Swimming in a world of tears,
Have comfort in this one thing, Mother—
Just know that the angels came.

I Am Free of My Past

I am made free of the chains of my past
I'm no longer held hostage within their grasp
The stronghold has loosed its hold
I'm made free in mind, body, and soul
I am no longer bound as his prisoner
I am free and being freer
The residue of his power has long been gone
I no longer sing his captive song
I've words to sing a brand-new song
I've long awaited this freedom moment
I no longer live in my past torment
I am wearing my freedom garment
Freedom, my long-awaited friend
My soul's been lifted, loosened from my past's descending ties
I'm as an eagle in mount to fly
Surely I am made free from the bondage of my past
No longer haunted by its ugly memory
My past no longer holds me tightly
Like a lover embraced in her lover's arms
I was subdued and tangled in my past's charms
The past held me tightly
Depression surrounded me while my past haunted me
And so, oh Lord, I call to thee
Come, oh Lord, and rescue me
Oh, king Jesus had the key
He loosed the grips and made me free
No more chains holding me
God, my help, delivered me

I Am God

I am God of oceans and of seas,

The revealer of all life's mysteries.

I placed the sun in the sky;

I hung the moon up on high.

I dug the valley deep down low;

I made the mountaintops capped with snow.

I made the greenest hillside meadows.

I made the waterfalls crisp and clean.

I made the grass the greenest green.

I made the earth of dust and clay.

I am the truth, I am the way.

I made the night darkness stars to shine.

I made the rocks and diamond mines.

I made the pearls of the seas.

I made the tallest cedar trees.

I made the busy honeybees.

I created the Universe all intact;

I am God—that's a fact.

I Am My Father's Daughter

Childhood memories long erased
When last I saw my father's face.
But, oh, I found it yesterday as I looked into the looking glass—
I found my father's face at last.
I found his face in mine;
How brightly it did shine.
I saw his face anew,
A quick glance of déjà vu.
Father, how I look just like you.
It was you I saw in me;
The color of your skin,
An exact replica of the skin I'm in.
I am you; I am the flesh and blood of yours.
Our blood runs the same, of course,
But yet you deny me—
My eyes that shine so bright,
My smile of fresh delight.
I am beautiful; I am yours—
Spirit and body, all of me.
It's in me; it's you I see.
It's plain and simple, no mystery.
You are my father; I am your daughter.
I am yours, you see.
There's no denying, no more defying—
I am yours.
So surrender to this truth:
I am the seed that you produced.
To my natural father,
I am your daughter.

I Heard the Angel Sing

Awakening my spirit way down deep,

A place in my innermost soul.

I heard their voices of truth and serenity;

They sung to me from earth to eternity.

They sung a song like I've never heard before

From the brink of heaven's doors.

In heavenly, majestic voices, they sung in unison,

All of one accord.

Never missing a beat,

A sound so sweet.

They traveled through this body made of clay;

Felt like the birthing of a brand-new day.

Their voices seeped like living water to a thirsty soul.

They sing, "Hallelujah to the king, hallelujah to the king."

To the lion of Judah, the angels sing,

"Hallelujah to the king."

I Press

I'm pressing my way through life's circumstances,
Sometimes heavy and burdened down.
I won't give up; I won't slow down.
Sometimes I walk with tearstained eyes
With a thousand questions in my mind,
But to slow down or give up, I haven't time.
I must keep walking my destined road;
I must stay focused on the destined goal.
No one said this road would be easy.
No one can walk this road for me.
I must press with God's guidance;
He's the only true help I know.
He designed the road map and the directions I must go.
He is the keeper of my soul.
I must keep steady my pace,
Keeping a smile on my face,
Determined to make it by God's grace.
I may never be the swiftest
Or proclaim to be the strongest.
This one thing I am for sure;
I must keep pressing.
I'm destined to see God's face in peace.
If I should ever have to walk alone,
I'll keep pressing until I make it home.
The end of my journey … the master's throne.

I Will Dance

I will dance unto the Lord, for he has made me glad.

I will dance because I am free;

No more chains are binding me.

I will dance because I am healed;

I am walking in God's will.

I will dance because my heart is light;

Darkness gave way and took its flight.

I'm made new.

I give praise and thanks to you.

I dance because I'm blessed;

God has given me all His best.

I dance because the enemy can't harm me.

What praise and thanks I give to thee.

I dance because I'm living,

Because you're so graceful in your giving.

I dance the dance of victory,

For in you, oh Lord, there's no defeat;

You've made every demon retreat.

I dance at the sound of your word,

The greatest knowledge ever heard.

I dance a dance like David danced,

For your awesomeness astounds me.

I will dance unto the Lord.

I Will Run to Christ

Sometimes life makes me want to run away,

But where will I go?

To the Lord I pray.

He soon chased those thoughts away.

These thoughts cross my mind from time to time,

But where can I go?

In my heart of hearts, I do not know,

Though I think sometimes I'll run away,

Someplace where there's no familiar face.

Some secluded far and distant place.

I'll run from all that ever hurt and tried to break me,

From my enemies that tried to overtake me,

From friends that betray and forsake.

I think I'll run away from those that lipped they loved me,

While within their hearts they hated me.

I'll get away from all users and false accusers.

I'll leave all those behind.

I've felt like this so many times.

But I will stand still and run to Christ.

I'm Free

When hurt consumed me,
I could no longer resume me.
I just couldn't get back to being me.
Like a child abused,
I was subdued by hurt.
Like a prisoner in chains,
My soul was held captive by hurt.
Words couldn't explain the devastation.
I've never experienced hurt to this degree.
I just couldn't get back to being me.
Where to go? What to do?
I had no clue.
And so, dear Lord,
I come to you.
The art of forgiveness you taught me.
Freedom of mind and spirit you brought me.
Through the art of forgiveness my chains were broken.
It's you, oh Lord, I'll forever hope in.

If I Could Gather ...

If I could gather all of life's raindrops,
Would I have gathered me a sea?
The answer to this question's way beyond me.
Although the winds of life are blowing,
There's no way of really knowing
Where the winds of life will carry me.
If I could gather all life's sunlight,
Would I have made void the dark of night,
Only to experience days full of love, warmth, and light?
If I could capture the beauty of the rainbow,
Would I always have beautiful, blissful days?
If I could gather the stars that light the darkest sky,
Would I have gathered eternal life?

In the Heart of a Child

There's innocence and joy.

In the heart of a child, there's true love and forgiveness.

In the heart of a child, there's wonder and excitement.

In the heart of a child, there's peace and contentment.

In the heart of a child, there's faith and trust.

In the heart of a child, there's desire and fulfillment.

In the heart of a child, there's honesty and uniqueness.

In the heart of a child is what God desires in all of us.

Increase Me, Oh Lord

Increase me daily, oh Lord, with your spirit of love,
Love I can never have too much.
Let it flow from your bounty above.
Let the spirit of love multiply me with meekness.
Deliver me from all my weakness.
And add to me the spirit of gentleness, patience, long-suffering, and faith.
That I may walk upright and guiltless in your way,
That I may never judge another day and think myself right,
That I may walk humbly within your, loving guidance.

Let the Weak Say I'm Strong

Life and people sometimes make you tired,
Not to mention life's fiery trials.
And so your eyes flood with tears.
Nobody knows your heartache and your fears.
You try hard not to complain.
You bear the burden and the pain.
As you go to God on bending knees,
You pray, "Lord, help me please."
There's not an option for failure or defeat.
Keep on fighting; don't retreat.
You've kept your battle so discreet,
Never broadcasting what you've been going through,
Knowing full well in your heart that
Victory belongs to you.
Let the weak say I am strong.

Life Is but for a Moment

So don't put off for tomorrow what you should do today,
For tomorrow's distant sun may shine upon your grave.
So today, while you live, give all that you can give,
Love all that you can love,
Hug all that you can hug,
Giving all of you to someone else—
Someone who has lost his way.
You'll receive a great reward
Some distant future day,
For life is but for a moment.

Life's Hardships

Trials, tribulations, pain, and devastation
Life's adversities, crosses, and losses
Hurts and despair
They come not to impair but instead to make one strong
We're tried by life's fires
Life's heartaches inquire of us
What are we made of- hate, greed, envy, or strife?
We must be tried and proven in life
Whether we're a vessel of gold, silver, wood, or stubble
We're made strong in life's raging troubles
Shall you be found pure or an imitation of gold
Are you true to your soul?
Or are you playing a role?

Light in the Darkness

In the darkness of the night,
The stars still shine
Like uncut diamonds in the darkest mine.
As a matter of fact,
Does it matter how dark my way may be?
The light of hope lives down in me.
Faith and hope help me see
Beyond the darkness surrounding me.
The light of love surrenders me
To a place of stability.
By darkness' power, I am never subdued,
For God's light of love is my fuel.

Love Goes a Long Way

Real love—nothing can kill it.
It adheres to the spirit.
The soul reveals it way down deep.
It shines above all that troubles me.
Love touches and frees me,
That I may be free in the spirit.
Real love knocks at the door of my heart.
Real love is sweet.
Sweeter than the honey seeping out of the beehive,
Real love touches all and makes it alive.
It's a feeling of warmth and tranquility,
Chasing the billowing clouds from my mind,
Renewing joy and gladness in my soul.
A little love goes a long way.
A card from my love,
I'm being thought of.
A call from my friend,
No false pretense,
Real love never ends.
A simple hello,
Just wanted you to know.
A little love goes a long way.
A hug or a kiss,
Leaving a feeling of bliss.
Love so beautiful to be felt
Makes one's heart melt.
Brings a smile to one's face,
Makes life's pain go away.
If just for one moment,
Love … just let me own it,
Thereby letting me know
I am never alone.
A little love goes a long way.

Love's Splendor

Love's a many-splendored thing.
Of its praises people sing.
And, oh, on ears it sounds so sweet
When sung in purity with no deceit.
Though from lips of guile it's sometimes spoken
To gain some timely gift or token.
From this great word
True hearts are broken.
Yet in its truth, most yet hoping
To find a love so careful chosen.
A love that lasts throughout the ages
Through life's seas and tempest rages.
True love withstands any tasks,
No matter what this life may ask.
True love so sound,
A gift from heaven.
From this great word the worlds were framed,
Great beasts were tamed,
Faint hearts were changed.
Through this great word "love," life was given
By the nails so deeply driven.
Love's a many-splendored thing.

Make Me a Masterpiece

You're creator and master;

I'm in need of repair.

You're God all powerful; I'm in need of your care.

Take your hands of craftiness.

Mold, break, and make me and bind me with glue.

Hold me in perfect place,

Refinish, and make me new.

Take out the old; renew my soul.

Renew the right spirit within me.

Remove the billows from my mind.

Make me, oh Lord, your creative design.

Make me the me that you have in mind.

Make me inside as beautiful as I can be.

Make me a valuable art piece for all to see.

That to the potter we all must go

And place your autograph, signed and sealed.

That, in me, you glory shall be revealed.

I'm that masterpiece designed by God, signed and sealed.

Material Things, All Vanity

This world's system carried away by material things.
The glitz, glamour, and worldly clamor.
Vanity advertised in the songs they sing;
It's all about the bling, money, and superficial things.
The finest of home, clothes, and cars,
A desire to live large like the stars.
The finest of things, all vanity.
Good health, a sound mind, and love mean everything.
Things can't renew a dying soul
When the storms of life take their toll.
Things can't turn back the hands of time,
Can't give renewal of the mind.
Things can't change a world that's gotten cold,
Where many deceive for wealth and gold.
Things can't console a broken spirit.
When life's cold and empty, things can't feel it.
When ravaged by disease, things can't heal it.
Things can never be to one a dear friend,
Can't walk with you through thick and thin.
Things don't possess a soul like man,
Have no mind to understand,
Can never do what mankind can.
Things can't encourage when one does good.
Wouldn't it be nice if things could?
There are great issues and problems things can't fix,
Like the prejudices of men that makes them sick.
Things won't go with you in the grave.
You will leave this world just like you came.

Maternal Mother

Conceived by her through by a seed,

Her body supplied my every need.

Through blood and water I was fed; inside her belly was my bed,

Her pelvis a pillow for my head.

Her body kept me warm and safe, nestled in a perfect space;

Although cradled in a limited space, her vital organs I embraced.

Her heart so big I heard it pound.

How it beat an awesome sound; how it echoed all around.

Maternal mother, there is no other,

Besides the Lord, no greater lover.

She carried me for nine long months.

I developed heart and lungs, ten tiny toes, a cute little nose.

I lived in her; she was my clothes.

A life within a life, a body within a body,

This miracle of life you see,

The greatest gift you gave to me.

This debt of love I'll forever owe,

For through God and Mother I became a living soul.

Me

The only person I want to be is me.

For none can be me better than me,

Being who God created me to be.

To imitate or emulate is fine, but these are not truly mine.

By my own DNA, I am defined always tracing back to me.

For in me I am truly free.

Some go through life not satisfied with who they are,

Never realizing we're all stars.

We can all shine.

My light defines me,

The light in my soul.

The soul controls who I am inside.

Not the outer but the inner me completes me.

I'm more than this fleshly skin that I'm in.

I'm more than flesh and blood.

It's me my entire makeup that I must love.

I can never love anyone else if I cannot first love myself.

Mercy's Presence

I felt His mercy the other day
Like a mother's warm embrace.
A gentle kiss upon my face
Like a sunlit summer day.
Like the springtime summer bloom,
Its awesome presence fills the room.
God's enduring mercy shines so bright
Like the stars that shine at night.
When my soul was burdened down,
I felt mercy all around.
It planted my feet on solid ground.
Mercy's voice clearly said,
"Lift up thy countenance; lift up thy head.
Be strong and courageous—go ahead."

Mother

It's a small word with such great meaning:
Mother, a rock of stability,
A teacher of humility.
She's a world of information,
An example and demonstration.
Mother—
She loves with no reservation
Her children, her first obligation.
Mother—
She's a friend among all friends.
She's honest with no false pretending.
To the needs of others she's always attending.
Mother—
She's always busy doing something.
She's a warrior, a woman of faith and virtue.
You're the root from which I stem.
I see you in me
And me in you.
Mother—
I have learned from the best
How to weather life's greatest storms and test.
Under your guide I learned direction.
By your word and hand I learned correction.
You will always be my soul's inspiration.
Mother—
I will honor you throughout all my life's duration.

My Heart Beats

Tick tock like a clock, she beats to the rhythm of life,

My heart like a mechanical machine.

Uniquely placed inside my chest, she beats a rhythmic sound.

A sound that plays on and on

Like the sound of the orchestra,

Her tune is perfect.

Following the pattern of maker and conductor, she beats.

She's magnificent in her construction;

Praise to the maker who has no malfunction.

A complicated organ she is;

Every blood vessel, valve, and vein, she beats.

Like a drummer, she strikes her notes.

She's holds life within a soul.

"Oh, the power the heart holds."

My heart just keeps on beating.

Through life's tasks, she beats through it.

Through sunshine and rain, she beats.

Through heartaches and pains, she beats.

Through seconds and hours, she beats.

Through days, week, months, and years, she beats.

Like an engine that drives me, she beats.

I am alive; she beats.

My Journey

I've embarked upon a journey.

I'm releasing all haters and false embracers.

Upon this journey, I've no room for the cowardly backbiter,

That slander behind my back

That opposes and attacks.

I cannot walk with selfish users

Or those love abusers.

On my journey, I'm separating from toxic friends, foes, and family.

Those that walk with me but aren't for me

I cannot take with me.

I will not be hindered, stopped, or slowed down,

For I'm treading new territory and ground.

All that God has for me I will receive

A new anointing, God's appointing.

God's lifting me up above all opposition,

I'm in a new position.

My life's in new transition.

There's a plan and purpose on my life.

I give up all to walk with Christ.

My Testimony

On October 10, 2007, I was in a horrific accident one Tuesday night on my way to church, along with my daughter and a few more passengers. I was in the passenger seat in the front of the vehicle. The driver lost control of the vehicle and crashed into a fence. Everyone had minor injuries and managed to exit the vehicle. I tried to but noticed I was pinned to the passenger seat. I was impaled by an eight-foot-long four-and-a-half-inch-wide pole, which proceeded through my right side, through my back, and through my seat. I was airlifted to Broward Trauma Center in Fort Lauderdale Florida, and underwent surgery immediately. My recovery took a little less than a month. I am a miracle. Therefore, I am eternally grateful for my life, and I'd like to spend the rest of my life encouraging others and being grateful to God for sparing my life and family from what could have been.

Our Daily Bread

Give us this day, our daily bread.
Keep in remembrance all you've said,
That we may walk by your word every day.
"Help us, dear Lord," in my heart I pray.
Allow your words to live in our souls and hearts
And grant us forgiveness in each day we start.
Give us this day, our daily bread.
Your words, the greatest inspiration,
Our only soul salvation.
The greatest words ever read,
Spoken by you, written in red.
We cannot live by bread alone
But by the living bread from our Father's throne.
We all like sheep have gone astray.
Lead us, Lord, back to your way.
Give us this day, our daily bread,
Which heals the body, spirit, soul, and mind.
Amen.

Picked by You

Flowers in the field,

They come in an array of colors, shapes, and sizes.

In the field of life's flowers,

You chose me.

It was I that caught your eye and attention.

I was the one you chose;

It was to me that you proposed.

Asking for my hand,

You promised to be a faithful man

By giving me a wedding band.

That band stands for a unity never ending.

You plucked me from my field of standing.

Plucked from my family; planted in yours.

Adding to your family tree,

God united you and me

With our love destined to be.

I am that flower,

And so by your side I stand,

Pronouncing to all

That you're my man

And I'm your woman.

Through dark and light hours,

Through many anniversaries and flowers,

We will stand hand in hand,

This unity God ordained and planned.

Through sickness and health,

Poverty or wealth,

We're together blessed

In life, in death.

Praise Ye the Lord

Everything that has breath, praise the Lord.

The king of the jungle lets out His roar.

The birds sing as they soar.

The beauty of praise I adore.

God's awesome power none can ignore.

The magnificence of His powerful hand

Is seen by eyes throughout the land.

Praise the Lord, all of man.

Praise the Lord, all ye lands.

Rain that falls from the clouds,

Praise His name, clear and loud.

Volcanoes erupting, spitting lava and ash,

Give praise to the Lord.

Stormy winds a-blowing, waterfalls a-flowing,

In all its beauty showing, the stars at night glowing,

The moon bowing by day, the sun bowing by night,

Let everything praise the Lord.

Prayer Changes Things

Swelled with tears, I could hardly breathe.

A sincere prayer set my heart at ease,

Sent to me a settled peace

Like a subtle summer breeze.

Prayer, like a sunset after a long hot summer day,

Brought tranquility and healing grace.

Prayer, it eased my troubled mind.

Prayer, it's heaven's antidote for all that binds.

Prayer, a remedy for all that ails.

Sincere prayer always prevails.

Rainy Days

The skies turn gray as the rain falls, hitting the ground,

Pitter-patter, lightning flashes, thunder crashes.

The rains came so suddenly, falling from heaven's sky,

Beating upon all like a drum.

Falling on you, falling on me,

Falling for hours, life's outpour of showers.

Rainy days.

Without the rain, there would be no flowers.

No lakes, no streams,

No splendor of grass of the greenest green.

No lilies growing on the hillside meadows.

So don't mind the rain dominating the sun

To create life's beautiful rainbow—what a show.

What a beautiful sight, most assuredly,

Placed in the firmaments for all to see.

So go ahead, rain, fall on me.

I will dry like life's rains; they will subside.

Just as life's rain must fall and beat upon my flesh,

Like the sun, I will shine and rise again.

I will shine beyond the clouds.

I will triumph beyond the rains.

I will with joy shine again.

Reach

I must reach beyond what I can see,

Believe more than what my fleshly mind is telling me.

In faith there is a greater me.

Through Christ I have true victory.

There's more in life I must achieve.

In the Word of God I believe.

So I reach beyond life's constraints,

So believe in your heart and never faint.

Safety in His Arms

Life brings to us another storm,
Seemingly without a warning, uninformed.
Somehow we manage to fight our way through
With God's guidance and His truth.
We are anchored by His grace.
Through tempest winds, His arms embrace.
He keeps us steadfast, standing upon solid ground,
His love and mercy always surrounds.
When the storms of life seems to flood my soul,
When the billows try to take their toll,
I'm sheltered safely within His fold,
For He's the shepherd of my soul.
Though life brings to us many storms,
We are sheltered safely within the Master's arms.

Sampson Bennett

As I glance out of an open window, it hit me you're really gone.

Your house is empty; you are no longer there.

The thought of losing you was truly hard to bear.

You're no longer lying in the grass.

No longer basking in the sun.

A loyal friend, you were one.

The family's pit bull, Sampson.

The silence is felt in our souls.

If heaven has a place for dogs, surely you will go.

We miss your presence every day.

We weren't prepared to see you go away.

You were such a loyal friend.

You will be remembered to the end.

We remember your brown and shiny coat.

Your eyes of hazel brown; your temper a fresh delight.

Your bark's been silenced in the night.

You were truly a family member.

You will always be long remembered.

Shine

Let the light of love shine
Chase the billowing clouds from my mind
Shine in me your awesome glory
You are the author of my story
Shine deep down in my soul and heart
Shine in me, your work of art
Shine way down deep, way underneath
Shine your light upon all that's hidden
Shine on all that needs to be fixed
Shine upon my troubled mind
Lord and healer of all time
Shine in me, oh Lord
I can't make it without you
Without your direction, there is no clue
Shine your love upon my face
Strengthen while I run this race
Shine in a world that's on a downward spiral
Shine in me, life given revival
And let me shine within your glory
Let me shine above my situation
By your anointing, send inspiration
Shine, allowing me to stand the test of time
In this dark world, let me shine
Shine upon all that try to bind and hold me fast
Do it, Lord, just as I asked
Shine above this flesh that's made of clay
And let me walk within thy way
Shine in me, shine through me, shine all around me
Let your awesome power shine
Let the light of God shine

Sing a New Song

There's song of gladness in my heart,

To the world, let me impart.

Let me sing a song of love,

Its notes and rhythms from above.

Sing with me this brand-new song.

All the world, sing along.

A song of peace and tranquility,

This is what the whole world needs.

A song to make one glad,

To lift the burdened and the sad.

A song to make the whole world bright.

A song of unison with love and peace, let's unite.

A song anointed and spirit filled

With love and compassion, let us yield.

A song never ending

With love's lyrics, sing on and on.

Sisters at the Mall

Today with my sisters at the mall,

Oh, my lord, we had a ball.

We laughed, talked, and ate together.

Days like these should last forever.

We saw so many beautiful things;

We admired clothes, hats, shoes, and diamond rings.

"You know, we girls like to bling."

We were having so much fun;

Three sisters expressing genuine love.

I know God was smiling up above.

Spring Has Arrived

Once again, spring has arrived
At her appointed time.
God commands each season.
Spring has taken her place,
Settling in upon God's grace.
She has shown her beautiful face,
And, oh, how beautiful are her clothes.
The season of spring has settled in;
The beauty of her presence is felt within.
What a beautiful springtime day;
Winter's chill has gone away.
"It's springtime, it's springtime,"
The robins seem to sing,
Flying in on open wings.
She anxiously waits to build her nest,
Proudly showing off her breast.
Thanking God for the spring,
Her feathered friends chirp and sing.
The beauty of spring is ushered in;
Winter's freeze has come to an end.
Springtime flowers will soon come into bloom.
Pansies and roses will show off their faces.
And, oh, how beautiful they will be
In an array of colors for all to see.
Spring has surely arrived;
There's a brightness in the sky.
"Springtime, springtime has arrived."
Through the bitterness of winter, all survived.
Spring has brought with her brand-new life.

Stay True to the Vision

There's a charge of greatness placed on your life;
Your visions and dreams seem bigger than life.
Though the vision seems limitless,
Though the price tag high,
Encountering some jealousy, some envy, and strife.
The vision and mission must be accomplished through faith,
For in possessing the vision, opposition is great.
Though the vision seems uphill, steady, and long,
Be very courageous, faithful, and strong.
In staying true to the vision, you will sing victory's song.
Remember to lean on God's mighty arm.
Be a good soldier; keep marching on.
I can imagine your struggle, hard work, and pain,
Just keep in remembrance your work's not in vain.

Thank You, Lord

Thank you for the shift in the atmosphere.

Thank you for the pleasant breeze that dried my tears.

You calmed my fears and caused my storm to cease.

You set my soul at ease.

You relieve me with a blast of fresh air.

You proved to me you care.

Oh, magnificent father, you are always there.

You appointed an appointment with time;

You're the great divine.

You heard my heart's request,

All the way from heaven above.

Oh, how great is your love.

Thank you, Lord.

You smooth out the rough places,

Disappointed my enemies' faces.

My heart is filled with awe.

Within your love there is no flaw.

For when my enemies waged war against me,

A host of angels took charge for me.

Thank you, Lord, for you're more than the world against me.

The Big Blue Sky

Who can measure the big blue sky?

Who is it that can tell just how high?

Who can tell its length?

Who can measure how wide?

It stretches beyond seeing eyes

It goes on for miles and miles

Ascending above the highest mountains

Descending upon earth's great fountains

It seems to connect to the clear blue sea

Its beauty forever astounding me

The clear, big blue of the sky

Releasing rain and scattered dew

It shares its glory with the clouds of white

Making room for the bright sunlight

Oh, what beauty the sky beholds

It's a wonder to every soul

I've watched its beauty with childlike eyes

It yet astounds with much surprise

It brings to us hail, snow, sleet, and rain

You're a many-splendored thing

The Good Shepherd

I'm a sheep within His fold;
He's the keeper of my soul.
He's my help in time of need.
My hungry soul my shepherd feeds.
Guides my feet along life's way;
You're my help—to you I pray.
Keep me humble at your feet.
This the highest place for me;
Lord, let my soul seek after thee.
Without you, Lord, where would I be?
Without you, Oh Lord, there is no me.
I'm in constant search of thee.

The Infamous Gossiper

The gossiper is much like a garbage and junk collector,
Gathering the latest news, local babble, and petty talk.
Yes, the gossiper loves meddling, chatter, and malicious talk.
Likes to gather news and repeat hearsay.
He has really nothing of value to say.
The gossiper has a built-in gossip detector.
He's a tattler of matters great and small.
Gathering news to discredit, slander, and make one fall.
The gossip, the news scandalmonger,
Just as sinful as the town whoremonger.
The gossip wears many names; let me name just a few.
Hope these name don't apply to you:
The tattling muckraker, the back-biting chatterbox, old sly fox.
That old gossiper never stops.
He's known for his talkative nature.
Spreading gossip is truly his flavor.
He's known as a babbler; he likes telling tales and wreaking havoc.
That old gossiper has such a bad habit.
That old gossiping chatterbox starts rumors and wars,
Going from house to house, door to door.
He will tell your secrets;
He just can't keep it.
He's a false reporter,
A truth distorter.
News flash: shut down the gossip and spread the gospel.

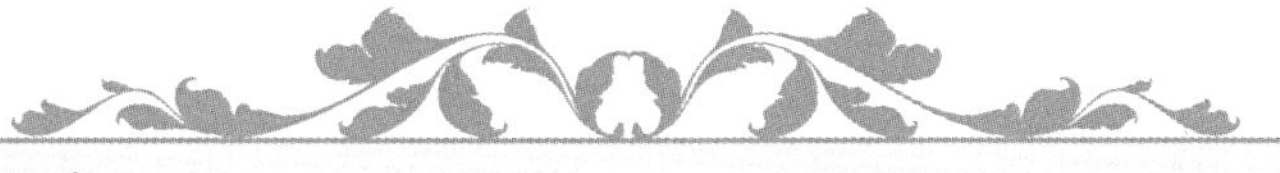

The Lord's Servant Made It Home

The Lord asked the angels, "Where's my servant I long awaited?"

The angels replied, "There she is, Lord. She's just entering heaven's gate."

"She's made it! She's here!"

All of heaven, applaud and cheer.

"Lord, your servant's made it home!

Her troubles are over, sorrows are gone.

She's now at rest; she's been given heaven's best.

Surely her soul belongs to you.

While on earth, she lived holy and true.

A faithful servant until the end.

The earth has lost a valuable soul.

She's now a citizen of heaven's role.

Yes, indeed, she will be missed.

But have comfort in knowing she's at home with the King.

Making it to heaven was for her a lifetime achievement and dream.

Yes, indeed, eternal life she has received!"

The Master's Fan

His fan is in His hand,
Sometimes forming a boisterous wind and wave.
We are shaken but not dismayed.
He fans away the husk from the wheat,
Separating the proud from the meek.
He fans us in the direction of His way,
Just as the potter forms His clay.
As the master craftsman turns up the heat,
Melting away from the gold all impurities.
As He purifies our souls in the heat of life's flames,
God is perfecting me.
I shall no longer be the same.

The Me in Me

There's a me in me that I should be
But there's another me that keeps that me from being free
It's that carnal me that cannot see
True victory in me being free
In me, I bear an enemy
Betwixt the Lord and I
That carnal me that needs to die
That carnal man with a capital *I*
Yes, he needs to be crucified
For when the spiritual man strives to soar
The carnal man begins to roar
I must be the me that God adores
The spirit man strives to live
The carnal man strives to kill
It's that carnal man that doesn't want to die
He fights daily to survive and outrun the spiritual I
The spiritual me stands like a tower
Like a rose, a beautiful flower
Planted by the rivers of living water
The spiritual I shall not be moved but will bear fruit in due season
The me that shall walk and never faint
Run and not be weary
I shall mount up with wings as an eagle
I must not live in the carnal me
The me that holds me captive
Like a prisoner bound in my own jail
Bound by my own mind
The carnal mind that binds
And so I go on fighting this war in me, myself, and I

The Road to Heaven

The road to heaven's eternal destiny is not paved with crooks and bends.

The road to travel is a straight one if you want to enter in.

The road will not be easy, and it may never be.

You can make it if you strive, so set your mind at ease.

The way to get to heaven comes with a compass and a guide.

The compass is the Bible, and the spirit is our guide.

We must follow its specific instructions to obtain eternal life.

There are no shortcuts or detours;

Straight is the way that you must go.

The road to heaven's destiny you may have to walk alone,

But remember while you're traveling,

You're getting closer to the throne.

Sometimes on this journey, you'll shed some bitter tears,

But one good thing about it: God is with you in all your fears.

He'll wipe away all tears.

So you just keep on traveling.

Keep heaven in your view.

There Must Be

In the absence of faith, there is doubt,
In the absence of love, there is hate,
In the absence of a forgiving heart, there's a hardened one,
In the absence of joy, there is sadness,
In the absence of humility, there is pride,
In the absence of unity, there is divide,
In the absence of communication, there is no understanding,
In the absence of sharing, there is no caring,
In the absence of patience, there is no peace,
In the absence of friends, there is no communion,
In the absence of truth, there is no foundation of life,
In the absence of unity, there is no harmony,
In the absence of a heartfelt smile, there is no gesture of kindness,
In the absence of faith, a world of despair is created,
In the absence of purity, there is violation,
In the absence of dreaming, life would be meaningless,
In the absence of music, there would be no song,
In the absence of opinions, there is no voice,
In the absence of a child, there is no joy and laughter,
In the absence of life, there must be death,
In the absence of fathers, there is a great void.

Through My Father's Eyes

If we could see through our father's eyes,
We'd love with humility,
Without selfish pride.
We'd share much love and abolish hate.
To all mankind, with compassion,
We would relate.
To all the hurting and those in need,
We'd express hospitality and never greed.
If we could see through our father's eyes,
We'd minister to the brokenhearted.
There would never be a moment of racial divide.
We'd have all in common and nothing to hide.
What a great nation and world it would be
When we look beyond faults and see our brother's needs.
If we could see through our father's eyes.

Twins

It proves that God is awesome when I look at you.

It's like looking in a mirror, seeing a reflection of two.

Identical twins—such uniqueness but a world of indifference.

Two gorgeous and blessed little girls,

You are God's creation, divine inspiration; you share a special gift and quality.

You arrived perfect and complete.

The two are so unique.

One just wouldn't do, so God created two.

I'm in awe of His great craftsmanship.

He's the master of creation, a master of design;

You're the product of His great and brilliant mind.

Two gifted and talented little girls—

What a treasure to the world.

Two identical, blessed little girls.

Two Made One

Two made one is how we've begun.
Don't throw it all away for moments of a stranger's time.
Don't fall for her beauty, body, shape, or mind.
Don't be swayed by her hips or one gentle kiss from her lips.
Two made one is how we've begun; don't throw it all away.
Though her hair long and fine, not tight and curly quite like mine,
Pleasing to the eyes and truly fine.
Two made one is how we've begun; don't throw it all away.
Though her skin's smooth as butter,
Not quite white but high yellow with a glow,
Don't let her snare your soul.
Her eyes like almonds, dark and large,
With a wink, she lights a spark.
Some are tempted to embark.
Two made one is how we've begun; don't throw it all away.
Don't let lust lead you astray;
Get a grip, go, and pray!
Though she may be stunning, manipulative, and cunning,
Look out, men—you should be running!
She bats her lashes—they're long and trim—while smiling with a cunning grin.
This kind determined to make men fall.
She says, "There's no harm. Give me a call.
I'd like to talk, that's all."
Don't take the bait—run away!
It's your marriage and family you will save.

Victory with Christ

I hear the marching of victory's feet.

He's coming to greet me and lift me up.

I shall mount the wings of victory.

Yes, my victory's come for me.

He's brought a victorious dance for my feet.

The power of victory's all over me.

It's in the clap of my hands,

In the praise of my lips,

In the posture of my stance.

Defeat and failure have no chance.

I will triumph with the Lord.

He's the victor I applaud.

I've sweet victory.

Through His name I shall never be ashamed.

A song of victory's in my ear.

I am joyous and full of cheer.

Yes, my victory's come for me.

I heard the marching of victory's feet.

He's come to apprehend me.

Yes! He's taken me as His own.

I'm surrendered in His arms.

I can't resist victory's charm.

Victory's come to change my life.

I'll forever have victory as I live and honor Christ.

Victory's initials are in my hands.

I'll forever dance my victory's dance.

We Are One

You are mine, and I am yours,

We're no longer a separate two,

The day and hour we said, "I do."

We are two made one flesh by God above,

The creator and author of our love.

Our love will long outlast hardships and trails;

We will keep our sacred vows.

Our love has weathered many storms;

I'm yet safe in your arms,

Never forgetting your brilliant charms.

You cause my sun to shine.

Our life's destiny is intertwined.

I am yours, and you are mine.

We're All One in the Same

We're all the same,
Different faces, different names.
Red, blue, black, or white,
We're all precious in God's sight.
We're of every race, creed, and color.
I'm your sister; you're my brother.
We all desire the best things in life.
We all have knowledge of Jesus Christ.
We're all fueled by rich, rich blood.
We all desire to be loved.
We're all one in the same.
We're people from all different walks of life.
We share the world day and night.
We all suffer loss and despair,
In search of one to love and care.
We're all the same.
We laugh, and we cry,
And one day, we live, and later, we die.
We're all in hope to receive,
The gift of God ... eternal life.

Wearisome Nights

Wearisome nights are appointed to me,
Those restless times when there's no sleep.
Lying in bed, my eyes open wide,
Communing with God as I lay there and cry.
Wearisome nights there's much on my mind.
What I feel in my heart is so hard to define.
Though I can't seem to put into words,
My sincere prayer and complaint I know God surely heard.
He knows my thoughts that cover me,
That crowd my head like the roaring seas,
Beating on me like the billowing breeze.
The God of comfort will give me peace.
He will put my mind at ease,
Though wearisome nights are appointed to me.
Even in my night season,
God is with me.

Welcome Home, Spring

We welcome all your things,
All the warmth and beauty you bring.
We're thankful for the cool, refreshing showers,
To water new birthing flowers,
For all the seeds that are growing,
For the gentle breeze that's blowing.
For the bounty of spring's harvest,
What a blessing spring has brought us.
Fruits and veggies all growing,
Brilliant, bright colors they are showing.
The richest greens and amber reds,
By your harvest the worlds are fed.
The sign of spring is everywhere.
Peace and tranquility flow gently in the air.
In the return of spring, God's power is seen on every vine and every tree.
Butterflies are flying; baby birds are chirping as they sit upon their nest.
Again, spring's returned, bringing her best.
By her great bounty all are blessed.

Who Knew?

Who knew that I'd be adrift on life's seas

With no way of knowing where the currents would carry me?

Yet with no direction, I believed.

Who knew that life's winds could be so strong?

Who knew the winds would blow so long?

Who knew that I'd lose dear friends along the way,

Some who'd promised that they would stay?

Who knew so many enemies would cross my way?

God always came to save the day.

Who knew God would meet me way out there on the open seas?

With love and guidance, he anchored me,

Caused life's stormy winds to cease.

He's in control of life's seas.

Who knew when dear friends rose up to become my enemies,

God would forever be there for me?

Who knew?

You Did Run Well

To my good and faithful servant,

Enter into my rest.

You've been faithful over a few things.

You've given me your best.

When life's race got hard,

You ran well and endured the cross.

You kept a steady pace,

Kept walking in the faith.

When the odds were against you, you continued to run.

When the storms of life descended upon you,

You didn't fall or slip.

You continued in the race.

When it seemed that you were losing,

You continued to run.

When others strove to beat and leave you behind,

You kept a determined mind.

Though many dropped out of the race,

You kept a steady pace.

A Beauty in All Things

There's a beauty of man
As he walks in His father's plan.
There's a beauty of every beast and bird,
Of every creature of land and sea.
There's a beauty of the moon and stars,
Of Venus, Neptune, Jupiter, and Mars.
All creation has its own beauty, obligation, and duty.
There's a beauty of all rivers, oceans, lakes, and seas,
Even in the smallest flowing streams.
"Glory to God!" they all seem to scream.
There's a beauty in the night's darkness, in its absence of light,
Giving way to the stars to shine so bright.
There's a beauty in each day that's born anew
As she kisses the moist morning dew.
There's a beauty to be found in each drop of rain,
For its essence of life its necessity sustains.

Printed in the United States
By Bookmasters